A Picture Book of
Martin Luther King, Jr.

A Picture Book of
Martin Luther King, Jr.

David A. Adler

illustrated by Robert Casilla

Holiday House / New York

For Joan Brathwaite
D.A.A.

For Carmen and Little Robert
R.C.

Library of Congress Cataloging-in-Publication Data

Adler, David A.
A picture book of Martin Luther King, Jr. / written by David A.
Adler ; illustrated by Robert Casilla. — 1st ed.
p.   cm.
Summary: A brief, illustrated, biography of the Baptist minister
and civil rights leader whose philosophy and practice of nonviolent
civil disobedience helped American blacks win many battles for equal
rights.
ISBN 0-8234-0770-5
1. King, Martin Luther, Jr., 1929–1968—Juvenile literature.
2. Afro-Americans—Biography—Juvenile literature.   3. Baptists—
United States—Clergy—Biography—Juvenile literature.   4. Civil
rights workers—United States—Biography—Juvenile literature.
5. Afro-Americans—Civil rights—Juvenile literature.   [1. King,
Martin Luther, Jr., 1929–1968.   2. Clergy.   3. Civil rights workers.
4. Afro-Americans—Biography.]   I. Casilla, Robert, ill.
II. Title.
E185.97.K5A63   1989
323.4′092′4—dc19   [B]   [92]
89-1930   CIP   AC
ISBN 0-8234-0770-5
ISBN 0-8234-0847-7 (pbk.)

MARTIN LUTHER KING, JR. was one of America's great leaders. He was a powerful speaker, and he spoke out against laws which kept black people out of many schools and jobs. He led protests and marches demanding fair laws for all people.

Martin Luther King Jr. was born on January 15, 1929 in Atlanta, Georgia. Martin's father was a pastor. His mother had been a teacher. Martin had an older sister, Willie Christine, and a younger brother, Alfred Daniel.

Young Martin liked to play baseball, football and basketball. He liked to ride his bicycle and to sing. He often sang in his father's church.

Martin (center) with his brother Alfred Daniel (left) and his sister Willie Christine (right)

Young Martin played in his backyard with his friends. One day he was told that two of his friends would no longer play with him, because they were white and he was black.

Martin cried. He didn't understand why the color of his skin should matter to anyone.

Martin's mother told him that many years ago black people were brought in chains to America and sold as slaves. She told him that long before Martin was born the slaves had been set free. However, there were still some people who did not treat black people fairly.

In Atlanta, where Martin lived, and elsewhere in the United States, there were "White Only" signs. Black people were not allowed in some parks, pools, hotels, restaurants and even schools. Blacks were kept out of many jobs.

Frederick Douglass

George Washington Carver

Harriet Tubman

Martin learned to read at home before he was old enough to start school. All through his childhood, he read books about black leaders.

Martin was a good student. He finished high school two years early and was just fifteen when he entered Morehouse College in Atlanta. At college Martin decided to become a minister.

After Martin was graduated from Morehouse, he studied for a doctorate at Boston University. While he was there he met Coretta Scott. She was studying music. They fell in love and married.

In 1954 Martin Luther King, Jr. began his first job as a pastor in Montgomery, Alabama. The next year Rosa Parks, a black woman, was arrested in Montgomery for sitting in the "White Only" section of a bus.

Dr. Martin Luther King, Jr. led a protest. Blacks throughout the city refused to ride the buses. Dr. King said, "There comes a time when people get tired of being kicked about."

One night, while Dr. King was at a meeting, someone threw a bomb into his house.

Martin's followers were angry. They wanted to fight. Martin told them to go home peacefully. "We must love our white brothers," he said. "We must meet hate with love."

The bus protest lasted almost a year. When it ended there were no more "White Only" sections on buses.

Dr. King decided to move back to Atlanta in 1960.
There, he continued to lead peaceful protests against
"White Only" waiting rooms, lunch counters and rest
rooms. He led many marches for freedom.

In 1963 Dr. King led the biggest march of all—the March on Washington. More than two hundred thousand black and white people followed him. "I have a dream," he said in his speech. "I have a dream that my four children will one day live in a nation where they will not be judged by the color of their skin but by the content of their character."

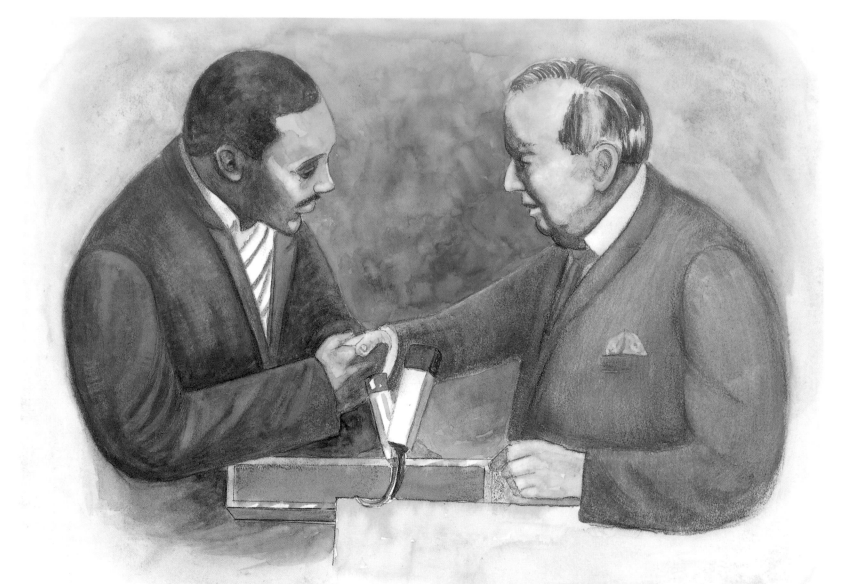

The next year in 1964, Dr. King was awarded one of the greatest honors any man can win, the Nobel Peace Prize.

The country was changing. New laws were passed. Blacks could go to the same schools as whites. They could go to the same stores, restaurants and hotels. "White Only" signs were against the law.

Dr. King told his followers to protest peacefully. But there were some riots and some violence.

Then, in April 1968, Dr. King went to Memphis, Tennessee. He planned to march so black and white garbage workers would get the same pay for the same work.

On April 4 in Memphis, Dr. King stood outside his motel room. Another man, James Earl Ray, was hiding nearby. He pointed a rifle at Dr. King. He fired the gun. An hour later Dr. King was dead.

Martin Luther King, Jr. dreamed of a world free of hate, prejudice and violence. Carved on the stone which marks his grave are the words, "I'm free at last."

IMPORTANT DATES

1929	Born on January 15 in Atlanta, Georgia.
1947	Ordained a minister.
1953	Married Coretta Scott in Marion, Alabama.
1955–1956	Led boycott of Montgomery, Alabama buses.
1963	Led the March on Washington on August 28 and gave his "I Have A Dream" speech from the steps of the Lincoln Memorial.
1964	Was awarded the Nobel Peace Prize.
1968	Assassinated on April 4 in Memphis, Tennessee.
1983	The third Monday in January was declared an annual federal holiday by the United States Congress to honor the life and ideals of Martin Luther King, Jr.